Acts

The Power Of The Holy Spirit

12-Week Study Guide
Brian Simmons

16
EasyRead Large

RHYW

Copyright Page from the Original Book

BroadStreet Publishing Group, LLC
Racine, Wisconsin, USA
BroadStreetPublishing.com

The Passionate Life Bible Study Series
ACTS: THE POWER OF THE HOLY SPIRIT

© 2016 BroadStreet Publishing Group

Edited by Jeremy Bouma

ISBN-13: 978-1-4245-5161-3 (softcover)
ISBN-13: 978-1-4245-5250-4 (e-book)

Cover design by Chris Garborg at www.garborgdesign.com
Typesetting by Katherine Lloyd at www.theDESKonline.com

Printed in the United States of America

16 17 18 19 20 5 4 3 2 1

TABLE OF CONTENTS

Using This Passionate Life Bible Study

The psalmist declares, "Truth's shining light guides me in my choices and decisions; the revelation of your Word makes my pathway clear" (Psalm 119:105).

This verse forms the foundation of the Passionate Life Bible Study series. Not only do we want to kindle within you a deep, burning passion for God and his Word, but we also want to let the Word's light blaze a bright path before you to help you make truth-filled choices and decisions, while encountering the heart of God along the way.

God longs to have his Word expressed in a way that would unlock the passion of his heart. Inspired by The Passion Translation but usable with any Bible translation, this is a heart-level Bible study, from the passion of God's heart to the passion of your heart. Our goal is to trigger inside you an overwhelming response to the truth of the Bible.

DISCOVER. EXPLORE. EXPERIENCE. SHARE.

Each of the following lessons is divided into four sections: *Discover the Heart of God;Explore the Heart of God;Experience the Heart of God;* and *Share the Heart of God.* They are meant to guide your study of the truth of God's Word, while drawing you closer and deeper into his passionate heart for you and your world.

The *Discover* section is designed to help you make observations about the reading. Every lesson opens with the same three questions: What did you notice, perhaps for the first time? What questions do you have? And, what did you learn about the heart of God? There are no right answers here! They are meant to jump-start your journey into God's truth by bringing to the surface your initial impressions about the passage. The other questions help draw your attention to specific points the author wrote and discover the truths God is conveying.

Explore takes you deeper into God's Word by inviting you to think more critically and explain what the passage is saying. Often there is some extra information to highlight and clarify certain aspects of the passage, while inviting you to make connections. Don't worry if the answers aren't immediately apparent. Sometimes you may need to dig a little deeper or take a little more time to think. You'll be grateful you did, because you will have tapped into God's revelation-light in greater measure!

Experience is meant to help you do just that: experience God's heart for you personally. It will help you live out God's Word by applying it to your unique life situation. Each question in this section is designed to bring the Bible into your world in fresh, exciting, and relevant ways. At the end of this section, you will have a better idea of how to make choices and decisions that please God, while walking through life on clear paths bathed in the light of his revelation!

The final section is *Share.* God's Word isn't meant to be merely studied or memorized; it's meant to be shared with other people—both through living and telling. This section helps you understand how the reading relates to growing closer to others, to enriching your fellowship and relationship with your world. It also helps you listen to the stories of those around you, so you can bridge Jesus' story with their stories.

SUGGESTIONS FOR INDIVIDUAL STUDY

Reading and studying the Bible is an exciting journey! It's like reading your favorite novel—where the purpose is encountering the heart and mind of the author through its characters and conflict, plot points, and prose.

This study is designed to help you encounter the heart of God and let his Word to you reach deep down into your very soul—all so you can live and enjoy the life he intends for you. And like with any journey, a number of practices will help you along the way:

1. Begin your lesson time in prayer, asking God to open up his Word to you in new ways, show areas of

your heart that need teaching and healing, and correct any area in which you're living contrary to his desires for your life.

2. Read the opening section to gain an understanding of the major themes of the reading and ideas for each lesson.

3. Read through the Scripture passage once, underlining or noting in your Bible anything that stands out to you. Reread the passage again, keeping in mind these three questions: What did you notice, perhaps for the first time? What questions do you have? What did you learn about the heart of God?

4. Write your answers to the questions in this Bible study guide or another notebook. If you do get stuck, first ask God to reveal his Word to you and guide you in his truth. And then, either wait until your small group time or ask your pastor or another respected leader for help.

5. Use the end of the lesson to focus your time of prayer, thanking and praising God for the truth of his Word, for what he has revealed to

you, and for how he has impacted your daily life.

SUGGESTIONS FOR SMALL GROUP STUDY

The goal of this study is to understand God's Word for you and your community in greater measure, while encountering his heart along the way. A number of practices will also help your group as you journey together:

1. Group studies usually go better when everyone is prepared to participate. The best way to prepare is to come having read the lesson's Scripture reading beforehand. Following the suggestions in each individual study will enrich your time as a community as well.

2. Before you begin the study, your group should nominate a leader to guide the discussion. While this person should work through the questions beforehand, his or her main job isn't to lecture, but to help move the conversation along

by asking the lesson questions and facilitating the discussion.

3. This study is meant to be a community affair where everyone shares. Be sure to listen well, contribute where you feel led, and try not to dominate the conversation.

4. The number one rule for community interaction is: nothing is off-limits! No question is too dumb; no answer is out of bounds. While many questions in this study have "right" answers, most are designed to push you and your friends to explore the passage more deeply and understand what it means for daily living.

5. Finally, be ready for God to reveal himself through the passage being discussed and through the discussion that arises out of the group he's put together. Pray that he would reveal his heart and revelation-light to you all in deeper ways. And be open to being challenged, corrected, and changed.

Again, we pray and trust that this Bible study will kindle in you a burning, passionate desire for God and his heart, while impacting your life for years to come. May it open wide the storehouse of heaven's revelation-light. May it reveal new and greater insights into the mysteries of God and the kingdom-realm life he has for you. And may you encounter the heart of God in more fresh and relevant ways than you ever thought possible!

Introduction to the Book of Acts

The book of Acts is the second volume in a two-book analysis of the Jesus movement by Luke. It picks up where Jesus' story left off in the Gospel of Luke by exploring the continuing presence of Christ on earth: the church. This inspired account of early church history will awaken your soul with transforming power and give you courage to be a witness for Christ wherever he sends you!

Dr. Luke offers a vivid portrait of the church's birth by cataloging the historical events in the movement of Jesus' early followers. It reads like a bestselling novel, chronicling the high-stakes adventure of major Christian leaders who carried the good news about Jesus throughout the Mediterranean world: from the disciples to early converts, to Paul and Roman officials; from the church's dramatic birth in the upper room to early persecution and martyrdom, on to Paul's dramatic conversion and imprisonment.

Luke masterfully weaves together characters and plots to tell this dramatic tale!

We've designed this study to help you explore and discover God's heart for the world through Luke's detailed historical analysis of history's most unlikely movement, the church of Jesus Christ. The truths Luke unveils in the book of Acts reveal how God is moving in the world today. So dive into this book heart first, to discover and experience the same fire that fueled the passion of early Christians two thousand years ago!

Lesson 1

The Church Is Born

ACTS 1:1–2:47

They were continually filled with praises to God, enjoying the favor of all the people. And the Lord kept adding to their number daily those who were coming to life. (Acts 2:47)

When life changes, we are bound to experience the stress and anxiety that spring from such change. You could argue the struggles the apostles faced during the early days of the church reflected the kinds of stressors we often experience.

They experienced a massive career change: from fishermen to movement-leaders. They navigated a world in which they were both immensely popular and persecuted. Their hearts were tested against money as people sold their possessions and laid the proceeds at their feet. Not to mention the gift of the Holy Spirit and a rebirth as the people of God!

It really is remarkable what the apostles went through in those early days! Yet through it all, God was with them through the power of the Holy Spirit. As a result, in the earliest days the church grew, was unified, and moved in power to spread the good news of Jesus Christ.

Yes, the apostles had their difficulties. In the end, what mattered most was that they also experienced God in a way no human had before. He was with them through the newness and change, birthing his church in all its glory!

Discover the Heart of God

- After reading Acts 1:1–2:47, what did you notice, perhaps for the first time? What questions do you have? What did you learn about the heart of God?
- Before Jesus ascended to the right hand of the Father, he instructed the disciples not to leave Jerusalem. Why? What did he promise them?

- Why did the apostles decide they needed to find a replacement for Judas?
- What happened that made so many people come running to the disciples in Acts 2? How did the people react to them? What did Peter say to them?
- Chapter 2 closes with a list of the things early believers were devoted to and experienced. List them.

Explore the Heart of God

- Jesus told the apostles not to leave Jerusalem, but to wait for the promised gift of the Holy Spirit. Why do you think it was so important to Jesus for them to receive the Spirit's power before they left to be his witnesses?
- Luke uses two words to describe the Holy Spirit's entrance into the disciples' lives. One means "filled inwardly" and the other means "filled outwardly." What do you think the differences are between these two experiences, and why are they significant for the life of the believer?

- Review Peter's Pentecost sermon to the crowd in 2:14–36. Knowing that most of the crowd were probably Jewish, why do you think Peter addressed them this way? Explain what he said in your own words.
- Our reading ends with a glimpse into the life of the earliest Christians in 2:41–47. Luke writes they were devoted to several things: teaching, fellowship, the breaking of bread,[1] and prayer. The result was signs and wonders, mutual provision, a good reputation in the community, and people coming to Christ. Explain how their devotion is what led to the results.

---

[1] Some believe this simply referred to shared common meals among the early Christians. Others argue Luke was referring specifically to the Lord's Supper, alluding to Jesus' own "breaking of bread" in his gospel. Others still posit it refers to both, where Jesus' broken body and shed blood was remembered during regularly shared meals among the believers.

Experience the Heart of God

- In Acts 2, the gift of power Jesus promised to give his followers was given with the coming of the Holy Spirit. How might it look in your life to consciously rely on his power every day, not only to obey and follow Jesus, but also to experience and share him fully?
- Prayer is a constant theme in chapters one and two. Clearly, Jesus and his disciples saw it as a necessary piece in preparing for what God would pour out upon them. Describe the role of prayer in your life.
- Another major theme in this reading is unity, found in verses 1:14, 2:1, and 2:42–47. Clearly unity was a major ingredient to God's work in the early church. How do you think it looks to help build unity in God's body today?
- How might it look in your life and in the life of your church to experience the heart of God through the kind of devotion we find in 2:42–47?

Share the Heart of God

- When Peter stood up to address the crowd, he retold the story of Jesus, beginning with the Jewish story. Why might this be a good template for sharing the good news about Jesus with your own world? How could you use it to share the heart of God?
- How might it look in your life and in the life of your church to share the heart of God in the way the early church did in 2:42–47?

CONSIDER THIS

Among the disciples were fishermen, accountants, political activists, and dreamers. There was nothing extraordinary about them until Jesus changed them through the gift of the Holy Spirit. Though them, the Holy Spirit birthed the church and Jesus continued his mission of rescue and "re-creation." Through them, the world was changed forever. Commit to carrying out the mission and message of Jesus' redemption in your own world, dreaming of specific ways you can share the heart of God.

Lesson 2

Miracles and Message of Mercy

ACTS 3:1–4:37

"There is no one else who has the power to save us, for there is only one name to whom God has given authority by which we must experience salvation: the name of Jesus." (Acts 4:12)

One of the most remarkable realities of Luke's two-volume series on the story of Jesus is the revelation that Jesus' followers are sent to do and teach what Jesus did and taught.

In Luke 9, Jesus commissioned his twelve disciples to preach about God's kingdom-realm and then demonstrate it through healing and release. Then, in the next chapter, he sent even more of his followers to do the same. And before he ascended to heaven, Jesus revealed his followers would bear witness to him and his reality of mercy all over the world!

Today's reading reveals the kind of miracles and message of mercy we too are called to bring and bear. Remarkably, it looks very similar to Jesus! Through the power of the Holy Spirit working through the early Christians, a crippled beggar was healed, the message of Christ's saving work went out, and believers overflowed with love for their community.

It's true: there is only one name who has the authority to save us. That name is Jesus. And, amazingly, we bear that name as his followers and children to bring Jesus' merciful salvation to a needy world.

Discover the Heart of God

- After reading Acts 3:1–4:37, what did you notice, perhaps for the first time? What questions do you have? What did you learn about the heart of God?
- How did the lame man respond to his healing? How did the crowds respond, and what did Peter say to

them about what happened, especially what had healed the man?
- Why did Peter and John's teaching and preaching anger the Jewish council so much? What did the Jewish council find against them in chapter 4?
- When the other believers heard what had happened to Peter and John, how did they respond? Then how did God respond?
- This section of reading ends with another description of the early church in 4:32–37. How is it described?

Explore the Heart of God

- No doubt, healing was a major part of Jesus' ministry. Remarkably, it was also a major part of the apostles' ministry! What does this tell us about God's heart?
- Why is it significant that Peter healed the crippled man in the "name of Jesus Christ of Nazareth" (3:6)?
- In what way was the crowd heir to the prophecies from Samuel onward, as Peter said in 3:24–25?

- Notice how God responded to the church's prayers in 4:23–31. What does this teach us about the kind of prayers God delights in, and his response to them?
- Wherever the early church went to proclaim Jesus, God backed them up with signs, wonders, and miracles—even supernatural jailbreaks! What does this show us about God's attitude toward us and his good news?

Experience the Heart of God

- When Peter and John were hauled before the council for questioning, Luke wrote that Peter was "filled with the Holy Spirit" (4:8) before answering their questions. What does this experience of Peter teach us about how we ourselves can experience the heart of God, especially when we are in trouble?
- Peter declared before the Jewish council, "There is no one else who has the power to save us..." (4:12). Why is this true? What does this

mean for our own experience of the heart of God?

- The Jewish council ordered Peter and John to stop speaking about Jesus. Reread their reply in 4:19–20. Why should their answer always guide our experience of God in the world around us?
- How might it look in your own Christian community to experience the heart of God as the early Christians did in 4:32–37? What practical steps can you take to foster such an experience?

Share the Heart of God

- Like Peter and John, many of us might not have money to share with people, but we do have Jesus and the heart of God! Why is this better? How can you always be ready to share like they were?
- Peter pointed to Jesus when the crowds came to him and John after they healed the crippled beggar. How should this example guide the way we share the heart of God with the world?

- The Jewish council was "astonished" at the courageous witness of Peter and John (4:8–12), because "they were just ordinary men who had never had religious training" (4:13). How should this encourage you in sharing the heart of God with your own world?

CONSIDER THIS

You may not feel like it sometimes, but you have been called, commissioned, and sent to do and teach what the earliest Christians did and taught. You are called to bring and bear miracles and messages of mercy! Consider how you can demonstrate and proclaim the reality that, through Jesus alone, people will find the salvation they so desperately need and desire.

Lesson 3

Suffering Disgrace for the Name of Jesus

ACTS 5:1–5:42

"We must listen to and obey God more than pleasing religious leaders." (Acts 5:29)

If you live in a Western nation (like America or Australia), there's a good chance you haven't experienced true persecution before. Sure, maybe someone has called you a name or ridiculed you for your faith. But you probably haven't been beaten, arrested, and jailed for it!

As we move through the story of the early church, things begin to heat up. More and more people believed in Jesus, and the church increased in numbers. But then early followers of

Christ began to suffer disgrace for the name of Jesus.

Jewish religious leaders were so jealous of the popularity and power of the apostles that they had them arrested, chained, and jailed. And after they were miraculously released, the same leaders beat them and ordered them never again to speak about the name of Jesus. Remarkably, the apostles counted it a privilege to have suffered for Jesus' name, and resolutely vowed to continue spreading the gospel of God's Anointed One.

May their example inspire us to listen to God rather than please others. May we be counted worthy to suffer the same kind of disgrace—all for the name of Jesus!

Discover the Heart of God

- After reading Acts 5:1–5:42, what did you notice, perhaps for the first time? What questions do you have? What did you learn about the heart of God?

- When Ananias and Sapphira sold their farm, what did they do? Compare this to what Joseph did in 4:36–37.
- Why did Ananias and Sapphira die? How did the early church react to their deaths?
- What happened when the people in the surrounding villages of Jerusalem brought the apostles the sick and those troubled by demons?
- What happened to the apostles after they were thrown in jail? How did they respond? How did Gamaliel respond to his fellow leaders' fury at the apostles?

Explore the Heart of God

- Early in the life of the early church, a wealthy couple, Ananias and Sapphira, pretended to give all of the proceeds of the sale of land to the apostles as an offering. And God struck them dead for lying about it! What should this tell us about the heart of God when it comes to being truthful with him?
- Why do you think more and more people believed in the Lord and

joined the early Christian movement as 5:14 says? How is 5:12–13 connected to this adding?

- When the jailor reported to the religious leaders of the apostles' escape, he said he found the jail securely locked and the guards standing by their cell. But when he opened the door, they were gone! How does this illustrate God's heart toward threatening circumstances in our life and those moments when he intervenes?
- Why do you think the Jewish religious leaders were so furious and had murderous intentions at Peter's reply in 5:29–32?

Experience the Heart of God

- Peter said that Ananias and Sapphira agreed together to "test the Spirit of the Lord" (5:9). How might it look in our world to test the Spirit of the Lord? How does this stand in the way of our experiencing the heart of God?
- How should the episode with Ananias and Sapphira in 5:1–11 impact how we live and experience the heart of

God, especially when it comes to money and our promises to God?

- After the apostles were beaten by the Jewish religious leaders, they rejoiced. Why? How should their response inspire our own experience of God in the world?

Share the Heart of God

- How should Peter's reply to the high priest in 5:29 inform how we share the heart of God in the world?
- Chapter 5 ends in a way that challenges us as we see the apostles rejoicing that they were counted worthy to suffer disgrace for Jesus. How does the apostles' response to persecution change the way you think about any persecution you might face?

CONSIDER THIS

Even though we may not be persecuted by threatened violence or imprisonment, we can be oppressed in subtler ways—often through being ostracized and pressured to conform to our culture. Close by praying for strength and perseverance to listen to and obey God rather than others. And pray for the persecuted church, who suffers true beatings, imprisonment, and death.

Lesson 4

A Powerful, Provocative Witness for Christ

ACTS 6:1–8:1

As they hurled stone after stone at him, Stephen prayed, "Our Lord Jesus, accept my spirit into your presence." He crumpled to his knees and shouted in a loud voice, "Our Lord, don't hold this sin against them." And then he died.
(Acts 7:59–60)

The greatest measure of leadership has never been how many followers you have, but how successful your followers become. This proves true for the apostles as well.

In Luke's account from today's reading, the apostles continued to expand Jesus' mission. The church had grown beyond the early days, adding to its number daily and multiplying exponentially. This expansion grew beyond the apostles' ability to manage all decisions, creating an opportunity for other leaders to rise. While their commission was initially practical and administrative, freeing the apostles to preach the Word of God, they also joined them in ministry.

Seven men were chosen, but we learn the most about Stephen, a remarkable man filled with the Holy Spirit. Like the apostles, he worked signs, wonders, and miracles, and bore prophetic witness to the crucified and risen Christ with power and authority. And like the apostles, his powerful witness got him into trouble. He became the first martyr for the cause of Christ after bearing witness to his name.

May Stephen's witness encourage us to be a powerful and provocative witness for Christ in our own world!

Discover the Heart of God

- After reading Acts 6:1–8:1, what did you notice, perhaps for the first time? What questions do you have?

What did you learn about the heart of God?

- What was the complaint certain Jewish believers had against other believers?
- What criteria did the apostles give for those chosen to serve in Acts 6?
- How is Stephen described throughout this reading?
- Why was Stephen opposed? What accusations did his opponents bring against him? What did Stephen emphasize in his defense before the council? What were his final words?

Explore the Heart of God

- Acts 6:1 indicates the church was growing faster than ever, but it's also the first place where any hint of disunity is mentioned. What does it say to you that the first instance of disunity was an issue of ethnicity, between those who spoke Aramaic and the Greek-speaking Jews?
- Why was Stephen's retelling of Abraham, Moses, and Israel's story important to what he was trying to

say in response to the religious leaders?

- Stephen distanced himself from his ancestry when he said, "You are always opposing the Holy Spirit, just like your forefathers!" (7:51). In what way was Stephen's Jewish audience following their forefathers? Why was that a bad thing?
- What happened to Stephen when he was persecuted and martyred? What should this tell us about the heart of God?

Experience the Heart of God

- It's easy to think little of service-oriented jobs, elevating those who teach over those who serve, but the apostles clearly saw this as a significant role. How does it change the way you think of your role in the church when you see how the apostles handled this situation?
- Stephen faced terrible false accusations before the court, yet he clung so tightly to Jesus that his face glowed like an angel! What manifests

in your life when you are opposed or falsely accused?

- Consider the life of Stephen, and the kind of experience with the heart of God he must have had to be able to endure persecution, yet share God's story and forgive his persecutors. How might it look in your life to experience God the same way by reflecting Stephen's example?

Share the Heart of God

- Based on the description of Stephen's life throughout this reading, what kind of person does it take to share the heart of God? How can you reflect this in your life?
- In the same way Stephen was opposed in his day, how might we be opposed in ours by sharing the heart of God?
- Stephen's passion and martyrdom for Christ provides a powerful life-example. How should it inspire and instruct your life when it comes to testifying about God's love and story?

CONSIDER THIS

Stephen's death didn't kill the church. As you'll see in the next lesson, Jesus' greatest persecutor became his most ardent voice. Despite the persecution that fills these chapters, they are still chapters of overwhelming hope. No matter what happened to the church, it only became more victorious! Ask God to help you apply this hope to your life today, and commit to fulfilling Stephen's legacy.

Lesson 5

As Persecution Increased, the Gospel Spread

ACTS 8:1–9:31

Saul agreed to be an accomplice to Stephen's stoning and participated in his execution. From that day on, a great persecution of the church in Jerusalem began. All the believers scattered into the countryside of Judea and among the Samaritans ... (Acts 8:1–2)

While we don't always understand the *why* behind life's tragedies, Paul is right: "Every detail of our lives is continually woven together to fit into God's perfect plan of bringing good into our lives" (Romans 8:28). We have such a clear illustration of this promise in today's lesson.

After the tragic death of Stephen, Luke recounts that a violent, merciless persecution came upon the Jerusalem church. But rather than killing the Jesus movement as Saul and the Jewish leaders had hoped, it exploded it! The believers scattered to the countryside and outer reaches of Judea and Samaria—taking the gospel with them, just as Jesus predicted (see 1:8).

As you engage today's reading, consider all of the people who wouldn't have been reached had Stephen not been martyred. There's Simon the sorcerer of Samaria. The Ethiopian government official. And then, the unlikeliest convert of all: Saul, an accomplice to Stephen's death and persecutor of the church, encountered this Jesus and was given a new name, Paul. God's former enemy was soon to become the most important mouthpiece of the gospel in the early church!

May we have the same confidence of Stephen before his death, knowing that God takes our bitter tragedies and spins them into gold-plated purposes!

Discover the Heart of God

- After reading Acts 8:1–9:31, what did you notice, perhaps for the first time? What questions do you have? What did you learn about the heart of God?
- According to 8:1, how did Stephen's martyrdom in the last lesson turn into a good thing? What things happened as the result of his death?
- What happened when Phillip confronted the pagan sorcery of Simon with the wonderful news of God's kingdom-realm and the name of Jesus?
- What did Simon try to do to Peter and John? How did they respond?
- Who was the Ethiopian Phillip encountered and what did he want?
- Why was Saul on his way to Damascus? What happened to him along the way? How did others respond?

Explore the Heart of God

- What does Stephen's death reveal about how God uses evil and tragedy for good and his mission in the world?

- Why was Peter so angry when Simon wanted to pay them for the gift of Holy Spirit anointing?
- How does the passage in Isaiah 53 that the Ethiopian was reading and Phillip explained connect and point to Jesus?
- Why is it significant that the booming voice of Jesus said: "Saul, Saul, why are you persecuting me?" (9:4). Who was Jesus talking about? How could Saul have been persecuting Jesus?

Experience the Heart of God

- While persecution and martyrdom are scary, what can we learn from Stephen and the early church's experience of it for our own experience of God's heart?
- Money and ministry have often been a deadly combination. What does the episode with Simon the sorcerer, Peter, and John teach us about experiencing the heart of God and ministry?

- Why might it be significant that when we are persecuted, Jesus is also persecuted? What does this show us about how Jesus sees us?

Share the Heart of God

- The apostles in Jerusalem sent Peter and John to lay hands on those who believed through his preaching in Samaria so they might receive the Holy Spirit. How important is it in your life to be filled with the Holy Spirit and to pray that others are also filled?
- Phillip went to a city where everyone was in awe of a renowned sorcerer who worked powerful signs, and then Phillip worked even greater signs than the sorcerer! How can God's power at work through Phillip give you confidence in your own witness for God?
- What can we learn from Phillip's approach with the Ethiopian man as we share the heart of God with others?
- How might you have felt if you were Ananias and God called you to share

his heart with someone like Saul, who had overseen Stephen's death and led a movement to destroy the early church through persecution? What should his response teach us about sharing God's heart?

- Paul's testimony proves that no heart is too hard for God to soften. Think of the person you know who is most hostile to Jesus' good news. How can you be a part of God's work in his or her life?

CONSIDER THIS

It's remarkable what God accomplished through the tragic death of his servant, Stephen. His death wasn't a tragedy; it was a triumph, because it was woven into God's perfect plan! The gospel spread, people found new life in Christ, and perhaps the greatest persecutor of Christ became his greatest advocate. May we remember that God uses life's great tragedies for his greater purpose and higher glory!

Lesson 6

God Does the Unexpected

ACTS 9:32–12:25

"Look what God has done! He's giving the gift of repentance that leads to life to people who aren't even Jews." (Acts 11:18)

God is a God of surprises! At every turn, the God-with-us God, Jesus Christ, was confounding followers and critics alike: he associated with a Samaritan woman, dined with tax collectors and sinners, and died like a criminal—before rising from the dead! God continued surprising the world in the early church by doing the unexpected: giving the gift of repentance that leads to life both to Jews and non-Jews alike.

For early followers of Christ, this would have been unthinkable because non-Jews were considered "unclean" by the Jewish law. Yet one day, Jesus appeared to Peter in a vision to show him God doesn't show favoritism, but treats everyone the same. Perhaps we need the same reminder: there is no group of people who are unclean and outside of God's rescue plan. He will continue working through us to spread his good news until he has gathered to himself people from every tribe, language, and nation.

As we read today's lesson, perhaps the best question to ask is: who is God leading us to minister to even if we are uncomfortable reaching out to them, even if we consider them unreachable?

Discover the Heart of God

- After reading Acts 9:32–12:25, what did you notice, perhaps for the first time? What questions do you have? What did you learn about the heart of God?
- What happened when Peter went up to the flat roof? How would you describe the experience in your own words?
- When Peter was brought to Cornelius' house, what did he realize about his

vision? What happened when Peter returned from meeting with him?

- How did Jewish believers react upon hearing the news that non-Jews received God's message and that Peter ate with Cornelius? How did Peter respond to the Jewish believers?
- What was the church's response to Agabus' prophecy about a coming famine?
- Peter was put into prison during an intense season of persecution by King Herod. What happened while he was there? What did Peter think about it at first?

Explore the Heart of God

- Luke records three conversions to Christ in chapters 8, 9, and 10. Each represents one of Noah's sons—the Ethiopian (Ham), Saul (Shem), and Cornelius (Japheth)—the sons through whom all nations began. Why is this significant?
- Peter's vision of the tablecloth and animals was quite remarkable! What

did it mean and how did it relate to and impact the apostles' mission?

- The Jewish believers were surprised when God also saved Gentiles (non-Jews), yet when a prophet foresaw a coming famine in Judea, those same Gentile believers determined to give whatever support they could to their Jewish brothers and sisters. How does this reveal God's heart?

- The Greek word *chrematizo* means "supernaturally revealed (imparted)," more than simply "called." It was first in Antioch where God revealed that the believers were "anointed ones," or Christians. How does this insight deepen your understanding of what it means to be a Christian?

- Up to this point in the book of Acts, we have seen an incredible diversity of miracles, and Peter's latest rescue from prison is yet another example. What can we learn from God's creativity in working miracles?

Experience the Heart of God

- Tabitha's story shows us that God cares deeply about his people. When was a time God miraculously intervened in your own life?
- Sometimes we don't fully understand what God is trying to teach us until later, like Peter with his vision. When was a time you had an experience like this, when God was telling or teaching you something, but you didn't fully understand it until later?
- In 10:34–35 we find the amazing reality that God doesn't show favoritism. He treats everyone equally. How does this verse deepen your understanding and experience of the heart of God?
- In 11:19–20 we see more of the fruit of Stephen's death. How should this inform and shape our understanding of painful experiences and God's heart toward those experiences?
- Luke writes, "The church went into a season of intense intercession, asking God to free [Peter]" (12:5). And God did! Yet when Peter showed up at a house where prayer for him

was taking place, they didn't believe it really happened. How should this experience shape our own experience of the heart of God through prayer?

Share the Heart of God

- Throughout Acts, there is often a profound response to hearing the gospel: crowds of people, even entire villages, become believers! How should this influence and inform how you share the heart of God with those around you?
- Peter's vision and experience with Cornelius was a watershed moment, not just in his life, but also in the history of the church and for what it meant for believers to understand that God no longer called anyone "unclean." How should this realization impact how we share the heart of God?
- Jesus is the Christ, or "Anointed One," but as the truth about Jesus was spread, believers also became known as Anointed Ones—Christians. This was because of God's power at work in and through them. How is

the power of God at work in and through you?

- How should 10:34–35 impact how we share the heart of God?
- Acts 11:24 reveals that, because of Barnabas' ministry, crowds of people were brought to the Lord. Who in your life does God want to be reached in the same way?
- How is the believers' response to the famine in Judea instructive when we share the heart of God with people tangibly and materially?
- Those praying for Peter didn't recognize when their prayers had been answered. How can you keep watch when you pray to know when God has answered you?

CONSIDER THIS

Sometimes we need a reminder that God loves everybody, that no one is "unclean"! He also wants to use us to reach the world like he used Peter with Cornelius. Spend some time considering the people your world might deem unclean and unreachable, whom God still treats with equal love and care—and how God might want to reach them through you.

Lesson 7

An Equal Message for Everyone

ACTS 13:1–15:35

"So listen, friends! Through this Jesus, the forgiveness of sins is offered to you. Everyone who believes in him is set free from sin and guilt—something the law of Moses had no power to do."
(Acts 13:38–39)

The earliest Christians bore a radical message for their day: the one true God was releasing salvation to the ends of the earth; salvation was for all people! It wasn't only for a select group of religious people; it wasn't reserved for the elite who could decipher secret spiritual codes.

No! Everyone who believes in Jesus finds release from sin and guilt. Everyone can have their lives put back together again!

This message was so radical and revolutionary that God's news about salvation spread throughout the entire region like wildfire—among the Jewish people as well as among the non-Jews. And why would we expect anything less, given this kind of news—news that was equal in measure and power for all people. As a result, early Christians won a large number of followers of Jesus throughout their region.

We need the same kind of message to go forth today. A message of equal salvation for everyone. A message that's unburdened by religious codes and customs, as the Jerusalem Council affirmed.

Discover the Heart of God

- After reading Acts 13:1–15:35, what did you notice, perhaps for the first time? What questions do you have? What did you learn about the heart of God?
- The miracles Luke recorded from Paul's ministry mirror the miracles he recorded from Peter's ministry.

Which miracles from these two ministries correspond to each other?

- When Paul and Barnabas went to a synagogue in Pisidian Antioch, the leader asked if they had a word of encouragement for them. In response, Paul said they were there "to share with you some wonderful news!" (13:32). What was that news he shared, and how did he share it? What did he say Jesus offers everyone?

- A number of false teachers from Judea told believers in Antioch they couldn't be saved unless they were circumcised according to the law of Moses. Why did they teach this, and what were they trying to do? What was Paul and Barnabas' response?

- In essence, the speeches of Peter and Jacob[2] before the council of Jerusalem boiled down to one theme. What was their message?

---

[2] "Jacob" is a literal rendering from the original Greek. This disciple is more widely known as James.

Explore the Heart of God

- Paul quoted many passages from the Hebrew Scriptures (Old Testament) when he preached in chapter 13. List the passages, and then explain why they are significant and how they relate to the gospel.
- The way Paul shared a word of encouragement with the Jews and non-Jews is important and followed how many shared Christ in Acts. How does the way Paul told Jesus' story reflect the methods used by Stephen and Peter?
- Compare how Paul and Barnabas were received by the Jews and how they were received by the Gentiles. What events were behind these different receptions?
- Why did the Law of Moses not have the power to set people free from sin and guilt?
- Why might the apostles' message to the people of Lystra be an answer to how we address our own multi-faith world?
- The insistence by the false teachers that believers had to adopt Jewish

religious rules led to the first significant church council, known as the Council of Jerusalem. What did they decide and why was it so significant?

Experience the Heart of God

- When the Holy Spirit came upon the first believers as pillars of fire, he directed them as the great pillar of fire directed Israel in the wilderness. Then we saw how he directed the church in Antioch, and then Paul and Barnabas. How have you seen God direct your life?
- Luke revealed that while the church of Antioch was worshipping in prayer and fasting one day, Barnabas and Saul received a calling from the Lord. What might this tell us about the way we experience the heart of God and his calling in our lives?
- How have you personally experienced the reality of the heart of God Paul shared in 13:39: "Everyone who believes in him is set free from sin and guilt"?

- It's clear that for Paul and Barnabas, fellowship with other believers and sharing their experiences was central to their ministry and Christian life. Why is church community so important to experiencing and sharing the heart of God? How have you found this to be true in your life?

Share the Heart of God

- Everywhere they went, Paul and Barnabas preached the gospel until it seemed that the only unbelievers left were those who wanted them dead. This is how determined God is to reach your heart. How can you become more determined to reach others with God's heart?
- Even though it took some explaining to help them receive it, many Jews celebrated every time they heard of God giving life to the Gentiles. How can you celebrate God's gift of salvation in other people's lives?
- When Paul and Barnabas went to the synagogue, they waited for an invitation to share "a word of encouragement." How might this

inform how we ourselves should share the heart of God?

- Acts 14:22 says that everywhere Paul and Barnabas went they "strengthened the lives of the believers and encouraged them to go deeper in their faith." What practical ways can you do the same in your own Christian community?
- How should the decision of the Council of Jerusalem and their letter to Gentile believers influence how you share the heart of God?

CONSIDER THIS

We see God orchestrating something wonderful throughout the book of Acts. The beginning chapters tell us repeatedly how unified the church was. And as Gentiles from diverse regions joined the faith, unity was still preserved. God still desires a unified church today. Ask him to help you do your part in building a unified body of Christ.

Lesson 8

A Legacy of Perseverance

ACTS 15:36–18:23

He argued the claims of the gospel with the Jews in the synagogue, and with those who were worshipers of God, and every day he preached in the public square with whoever would listen. (Acts 17:17)

As we continue joining Paul on his missionary journeys, perhaps one quality stands out above the rest: *perseverance.* The man kept going, despite hardships and setbacks! It's as if he didn't care what difficulties he faced, what punishments he endured, or what opposition confronted him. He simply pressed on.

This is the benefit of perseverance. A persevering farmer or gardener will eventually reap the benefits of patience and perseverance. The same was true of Paul. Because he persevered, churches were birthed from town to town. Though he was run out of most every city he visited, he left behind a legacy of churches that eventually thrived and became pillars of the worldwide church.

Paul's example and story should make us wonder what could happen in and through our own lives if we persevered as he did. What could happen if we talked about Jesus and his story, no matter what happened? What if we took risks so that people who do not know Jesus would meet him?

Paul didn't have to ask these questions. He lived out the answer.

Discover the Heart of God

- After reading Acts 15:36–18:23, what did you notice, perhaps for the first time? What questions do you have? What did you learn about the heart of God?
- Who was Lydia and what happened to her?

- How did Paul and Silas know God was leading them to Macedonia?
- What happened as a result of Paul releasing the girl from the spirit of Python?
- Why was Paul deeply troubled when he went to Athens?
- How does Luke describe the "more noble character" of the Jews in Berea?

Explore the Heart of God

- Before Paul took Timothy on as his ministry partner, he had him circumcised. Why? And what's a broader point we might glean from this regarding how we should minister to people?
- Acts 16:5 says, "All the churches were growing daily and were encouraged and strengthened in their faith." This statement is similar to those made of the early days in the Jerusalem church. What have you observed in Acts that might be keys to this environment of growth?
- Once Paul received a vision from God to give them direction again, they

"immediately prepared" to go (16:9–10). Why do you think Luke made special mention of their urgency in following the vision?

- When the earthquake set Paul and Silas free from prison, it was the third time in Acts that God freed his witnesses from jail (5:17–21, 12:6–11, 16:25–26). What does this teach us about God's nearness in times of trouble?
- Angered by Paul and Silas' message, jealous Jews in Thessalonica accused them of being troublemakers who "turned the world upside down" (17:6). What kind of life would it take for you to earn the distinction of having turned the world upside down?

Experience the Heart of God

- Acts 15:41 says that everywhere Paul and Silas went, "they left the church stronger and more encouraged than before." How do you think this looks practically and how can you make it true of your life?

- Interestingly, the Holy Spirit forbade Paul from preaching in one area, so he moved on. Was there a time in your life when you were prompted by the Holy Spirit to do or not do something? What was that like? How did it turn out? How can we discern the Holy Spirit's promptings, like Paul did?
- When Paul and Silas performed the miracle of exorcism they were beaten and jailed. Yet some remarkable fruit came out of their situation. What was it? And what does this teach us about how we can sometimes experience the heart of God in the midst of bad situations?
- Paul and Silas found the Jews of Berea to be of special character. How should we model our own pursuit of the heart of God after the Bereans?
- Why does Paul say the resurrection of Jesus is so important to our faith, and our experience of the heart of God?

Share the Heart of God

- The description of how Paul and Silas approached the people of Philippi feels so normal. They simply went to a house of worship and struck up a conversation (16:13). How can you follow their example to share the heart of God?
- The jailer of the prison where Paul and Silas were miraculously released asked them, "What must I do to be saved?" How would you answer this question if you were asked this question by someone in your life?
- Acts 17:1–3 reveals that Paul spent three weeks challenging Jews in Thessalonica "by explaining the truth and proving to them the reality of the gospel." What does this tell us about what's necessary when it comes to sharing the heart of God?
- The world Paul stepped into in Athens is similar to our own, with its multiple gods and faiths. Explain how Paul shared God's heart with them, and why his method should be our own.

- People will respond either positively or negatively to us when we share the heart of God. How should Paul's response in 18:6 inform how we respond?

CONSIDER THIS

As inspiring as Paul's life is, it can also be extremely intimidating. But why did Paul do what he did? Was he just a competitive overachiever? Was he superhuman in some way, capable of doing something we can't? No, he was just a man, but a man who knew Jesus intimately enough to know that Jesus was worth it all. Wherever you are with Jesus, ask him today to help you know him more.

Lesson 9

Celebrating Highs, Forecasting Lows

ACTS 18:24–21:14

"But whether I live or die is not important, for I don't esteem my life as indispensable. It's more important for me to fulfill my destiny and to finish the ministry my Lord Jesus has assigned to me, which is to faithfully preach the wonderful news of God's grace." (Acts 20:24)

Paul's life was a roller-coaster ride, a prefabricated path of ups and downs. This was especially true of the adventure we find in today's reading.

During his third missionary journey to the Gentiles, Paul led citywide revivals, saw a city's culture begin to transform, witnessed thousands of people set free, and planted more churches. Yet the Holy Spirit nudged him away from all this success: "It's time to go back to Jerusalem," he told Paul, adding, "By the way, you'll face chains and affliction there."

It would have been easy for Paul to protest this setback: *Wait a minute, God! Don't you see the good thing I've got going on here? Why should I go to where I know suffering awaits me?* But he didn't protest. He resolutely set his face toward Jerusalem and went.

Interestingly, it was while Paul was in prison that he wrote most of his letters in the New Testament. He may not have fully understood how following the Holy Spirit's leading to leave behind success would lead to such an incredible impact—the literally billions of people throughout history who have received and read his words in the Word of God!

Discover the Heart of God

- After reading Acts 18:24–21:14, what did you notice, perhaps for the first time? What questions do you have? What did you learn about the heart of God?
- Paul found believers in Ephesus who had neither heard of nor received the

Holy Spirit. What happened when they finally did receive him after they were baptized?

- What happened as a result of the demons beating up the sons of Sceva for misusing the name of Jesus?
- What was the cause of the "major disturbance" that erupted in Ephesus?
- Paul told the Ephesian elders he was compelled by the Holy Spirit to go to Jerusalem. What did he say awaited him there?

Explore the Heart of God

- What does the relationship between Priscilla, Aquila, and Apollos teach us about discipleship in the church?
- Explain the difference between John's baptism and baptism in light of Jesus. What do we receive from this new baptism that John's didn't provide?
- Acts 19:11–12 records some of the most incredible miracles in the entire book. What do we learn about our miracle-working God through such amazing testimonies?

- What happened to the sons of Sceva when they tried to use the name of Jesus? Why?
- Paul addressed three themes to the Ephesian elders: to maintain purity of faith in Jesus; to grow because of God's grace; and to guard our hearts regarding money. Why are these three themes so important?
- Paul tells the church leaders to guard their hearts, be true shepherds, and feed their flock well. Why does he urge this, and why is it important for other Christian leaders to follow Paul's advice?

Experience the Heart of God

- True authority comes from relationship with Jesus Christ, not just using formulas and techniques. Evil spirits know about the depth of our relationship with God. What should the story about the sons of Sceva teach us about experiencing the heart of God and name of Jesus?
- It's no surprise the gospel created such a disturbance in Ephesus, because the gospel is disruptive! In

what ways does it disrupt people's lives today? How has it disrupted yours?

- After sharing with his friends what the Holy Spirit said awaited him in Jerusalem, Paul said in 20:24 that it wasn't important for him whether he lived or died. What mattered was "to fulfill my destiny and to finish the ministry my Lord Jesus has assigned to me." What a powerful life-verse! How might your experience of the heart of God be impacted if you took the same attitude as Paul?
- In what ways have imposters invaded the church today, seducing people to abandon Jesus?

Share the Heart of God

- Throughout his journeys, Paul "brought words of great comfort and encouragement to the believers" (20:2). How can you share the same kind of comfort and encouragement with those in your life?
- Luke said Paul spent three months reasoning in the synagogue and taught for over two years every day

in Tyrannous' lecture hall about Jesus. What should this tell us about what it takes to share the heart of God and the story of Jesus?

- After two years of Paul's ministry in one city, Luke said that every person in the entire region had heard the word of the Lord. What could God do through you in the next two years?

- The love between Paul and his churches is so clear through Luke's stories of the Phillippian believers' "enormous joy" and the emotional exchange between Paul and the Ephesian elders. How can you cultivate a similar love between you and fellow believers?

- People had prophesied over Paul not to go to Jerusalem because of the danger awaiting him there. Yet he went, saying he was prepared to die for Christ! How should this encourage us to share the heart of God, despite whatever danger may await us?

CONSIDER THIS

Paul almost certainly didn't understand what he would do in prison or the impact it would have. He only knew that the Holy Spirit was leading him. Yet this was how he had lived his whole Christian life—following the Holy Spirit. By doing so, he had seen thousands find life in Jesus. How could he not help but trust God, even then? Like Paul did, renew your trust in God today to follow him wherever he leads you.

Lesson 10

It Wasn't Fair! Yet Paul Persevered

ACTS 21:15–23:35

While the crowd was screaming and yelling, removing their outer garments, and throwing handfuls of dust in the air in protest, the commander had Paul brought back into the compound. He ordered that he be whipped with a lash and interrogated to find out what he said that so infuriated the crowd. (Acts 22:23–24)

One of the most astounding things about Paul's missionary and Christian life was how patiently he endured his unfair mistreatment and trials. Case in point: when he came to Jerusalem, unbelieving Jews falsely accused him, unjustly beat him, and plotted murder against him.

Paul was left in prison for over two years waiting for this legal process to end. He suffered ongoing, escalating injustice, even from the hands of those charged with the very task of ensuring justice was served. It wasn't fair! Yet Paul remained steadfast, looking for any opportunity to share God's good news with anyone who would listen. He entrusted himself to God, knowing that man couldn't be his ultimate source of hope.

We have such a comforting, convicting example in Paul. There are times when life isn't fair and we may suffer injustice. Like Paul, our response to that injustice can be our greatest testimony. The testimony of our transformed life can be empowered by God to change others' lives as well.

Discover the Heart of God

- After reading Acts 21:15–23:35, what did you notice, perhaps for the first time? What questions do you have? What did you learn about the heart of God?
- When some Jewish leaders questioned Paul about rumors that he was

teaching Jews to abandon Moses and Jewish customs, how did he respond?

- Why was there such a disturbance in Jerusalem at Paul being sighted in the temple? What happened?
- When Paul addressed the crowd, describe what he told them in your own words.
- • Why did a heated argument break out at Paul's religious trial when he said he had hope in the dead rising to live again?

Explore the Heart of God

- Paul got into trouble with Jews from Turkey while trying to avoid trouble with Jews from Jerusalem. God warned Paul this would happen, yet sent him to Jerusalem anyway. Why would God have done this?
- Why do you think Paul reverted back to his Jewish customs by ceremonially purifying himself even though he had taught elsewhere that following such customs was no longer necessary?
- As Paul defended himself before the mob, he said that he was born in a city in Turkey, the same region

where God sent him to minister.
What does it say about God that he
sent Paul back to where his life
began?

- Why do you think the Jewish crowd
wanted to kill Paul when he said the
Lord told him he had been sent to
preach to non-Jewish nations? What
does that tell you about the crowd?
- When Paul was held at the Roman
headquarters at night, Jesus appeared
to him. According to an Aramaic
translation, Jesus told Paul to
"receive miracle power," while in the
Greek, Jesus tells him to "have
courage." Why were both necessary
for Paul's situation?[3]

---

[3] The Bible as we know it was originally
written in Hebrew, Aramaic, and Greek. In
recent years, there have been many new
discoveries regarding these original
manuscripts, especially the Aramaic ones of
the New Testament in addition to the
Greek. The Aramaic texts are an important,
added "lens" through which to view God's
original Word to us.

Experience the Heart of God

- When Paul stood to address the Jewish crowd, he basically gave testimony to his personal experience with Jesus and the heart of God. Spend some time writing out your own testimony.
- Paul got into trouble while trying to avoid it, was falsely accused, then beaten and chased by a mob who wanted him dead. Paul responded by ministering to them! How can you learn to respond just as admirably in difficult circumstances?
- Have you ever experienced a difficult situation and then Jesus gave you "miracle power" and "courage" like he did with Paul in prison? What was that like?

Share the Heart of God

- Even as he gave his defense to the mob that tried to kill him, Paul honored them by praising their passionate desire to please God. What can we learn from this as we look for opportunities to share God's heart with people?

- Paul's defense throughout his trials and before various authorities always included his testimony. What does this say to you about the power of your testimony as a tool for reaching the lost, regardless of how well you know the Bible?
- In 21:19 we see that God had accomplished a great deal through Paul's ministry among the non-Jewish people, even though he was more qualified to speak to the Jews, given his background. Who has God called you to reach for him, even though you may feel unqualified?

CONSIDER THIS

Next to the story of Jesus and his use of Scripture, Paul's personal testimony was one of his greatest tools! Not even the Jews could refute it. The wonderful thing about testimonies is that they're always growing, because God's work in our lives never ends. Your own testimony is one of your greatest tools, too. Take time today to remember God's work in your life and thank him for it. Then commit to putting your own testimony to work!

Lesson 11

Persecuted for Faith, Yet Filled with Hope

ACTS 24:1–26:32

"I am on trial because I believe in the hope of God's promises made to our ancestors ... But in spite of all this, I have experienced the supernatural help of God up to this very moment." (Acts 26:6, 22)

One of the most consistent, inescapable themes of Acts is persecution. Early leaders like Peter and John were arrested, beaten, chained, and imprisoned. This happened several more times. Eventually, some were even martyred for their faith, like Stephen.

What's remarkable is that even though these people suffered for Jesus, they celebrated their persecution and still had hope. Paul was one such person. After years of escaping harm, the religious leaders finally brought legal charges against him. They said he was a "contagious plague," accused him of sedition and stirring up riots, and claimed he tried to "desecrate our temple."

And all of it was false; they couldn't prove a single accusation! Of course Paul knew it, and he pled his case. Festus, the Roman governor, said he couldn't find one thing Paul had done wrong. Even the regional king and his sister said Paul hadn't deserved death or imprisonment.

Remarkably, despite these accusations and despite his imprisonment, Paul stayed the course. He used the opportunity to boldly share the revelation-light of Jesus' wonderful story. He also held on to hope. Not only the hope of Christ, but also the hope of God's help, protection, and support.

Discover the Heart of God

- After reading Acts 24:1–26:32, what did you notice, perhaps for the first time? What questions do you have? What did you learn about the heart of God?

- How did the high priest's attorney, Tertullus, accuse Paul before governor Felix? How did Paul respond, and why did he say he was being accused?
- How did Paul defend himself before King Agrippa?
- In 26:15–18, Paul shared a longer version of his conversion and testimony. What did Jesus reveal, and why was it significant to Paul's story?
- How did Festus react to Paul's testimony and defense? How did King Agrippa?

Explore the Heart of God

- Festus didn't have a credible purpose in sending Paul to Caesar, but God had a purpose in it. Why did God want Paul to go to Caesar?
- Why do you think Felix became terrified when Paul "spoke about true righteousness, self-control, and the coming judgment"? (24:25). How have you seen a similar response with others when they hear the gospel?

- What do you think Luke meant that Paul gave his defense "by the Holy Spirit"? (25:8).
- In what way had Paul not taught anything different from what Moses and the prophets had said was destined to happen?
- Compare the responses of Felix and King Agrippa to Paul's testimony. Why did they answer Paul so differently?
- What would have happened had Paul not appealed to Caesar? Why is this significant to the story of the early church?

Experience the Heart of God

- Joseph and Daniel in the Old Testament and Paul in the New Testament all experienced the same journey prior to speaking before the kings of their world—they became prisoners. How can we apply the lessons of their lives to help us during difficult times?
- One of the central guiding issues in all of Paul's trials is that he believed in the resurrection of the dead. Why

was the resurrection such a central issue in his life? What impact does it have in your life?

- Have you ever been falsely accused, like Paul? How did you experience the heart of God during that time?
- Paul told King Agrippa he had not been disobedient to what was revealed to him from heaven. When was a time God asked you to do something that might have been countercultural or others didn't agree with, yet you still experienced God's support and help?

Share the Heart of God

- Paul's imprisonment became his opportunity to teach many governing authorities about Jesus. What can you do to prepare to be God's witness and share his heart, regardless of your circumstances?
- When we stand for Christ and share the heart of God, there is a chance we will be falsely accused of all sorts of things, like Paul. How can his example encourage us to continue sharing Jesus, no matter what?

- Amazingly, the bad turn of events gave Paul the chance to share the heart of God before King Agrippa, his sister, senior military commanders, and prominent citizens. What does this tell you about the circumstances of our lives, and how God can use them to share Jesus with others?

CONSIDER THIS

Someday, many of us may face the same situations Paul and the early church leaders faced: persecution for our faith. Even if it's not physical or legal persecution, we may still be socially or emotionally oppressed. Do what Paul did—use those moments as a way to proclaim the heart of God and your hope in his help, protection, and strength.

Lesson 12

Paul Goes to Rome

ACTS 27:1–28:31

Paul lived two more years in Rome, in his own rented quarters, welcoming all who came to visit. He continued to proclaim to all the truths of God's kingdom-realm, teaching them about the Lord Jesus, the Anointed One, speaking triumphantly and without any restriction. (Acts 28:30–31)

Sometimes real life stories make for the best, most exciting stories. Paul's life certainly qualifies as this. As we read the final chapters of Acts, we have seen murder plots foiled, midnight escapes, political intrigue, dramatic courtroom scenes, multiple escapes from death, monster storms, angelic visitations, miraculous healings, and surviving a deadly snakebite.

The book of Acts closes, but it's not because the Holy Spirit was or is done with his mighty acts. If anything, the works of the Holy Spirit have grown, becoming more diverse and widespread—so much so that it would be impossible to record them all.

Those of us who believe in Jesus Christ have the same empowerment of the Holy Spirit as these mighty leaders from the early church. The Holy Spirit has not lost power over time, but is just as strong in you today as he was in them back then. As for Peter and Paul, the Holy Spirit's acts through them have been written for our inspiration.

Now, what acts will he do through you to inspire future generations?

Discover the Heart of God

- After reading Acts 27:1–28:31, what did you notice, perhaps for the first time? What questions do you have? What did you learn about the heart of God?
- Even though Paul was imprisoned under Roman guard, Paul was still cared for. List all the ways he experienced the heart of God on his journey to Rome.

- What happened when Paul gathered wood on the island of Malta?
- Why did Paul gather together all the prominent members of the Jewish community of Rome?

Explore the Heart of God

- Paul had faced death many times before the storm swept away his boat, demonstrating yet another time when God saved him. What does this show us about God's involvement in our lives?
- Interestingly, Paul told the pagan sailors and guards that God would protect them as much as him. What does this tell us about the heart of God?
- While moored on Malta, Paul healed the father of the island's governor, and then all the sick on the island. Healing is a prominent part of the sharing of the heart of God in Acts. Why do you suppose that was? What should we take away from this?
- Why was Paul right when he said the Holy Spirit said it well through Isaiah about the Jewish people in 28:25–27?

- While living in Rome, Paul "continued to proclaim to all the truths of God's kingdom-realm, teaching them about the Lord Jesus, the Anointed One, speaking triumphantly and without any restriction" (28:31). Why did he share the heart of God in this way? How similar or different is this from how Christians often share?

Experience the Heart of God

- Like Paul, we often experience trying circumstances, yet are cared for. Share an experience that was difficult, yet you experienced the heart of God in the middle of it.
- Luke noted that Paul was allowed to disembark in Sidon so that he might see his friends. Having been imprisoned for several years, this must have been a truly special experience for him even though it might seem small. What does God do for you that might seem small, but means a lot?
- Paul knew he carried an authority greater than either the ship's captain or the Roman commander. While he

submitted to earthly authorities to go on the ship, he knew when to exercise his greater authority. How can you grow in both your heavenly authority and your ability to know when to use it?

- Sometimes God puts us in situations to be an encouragement to others. In what way is 27:25, 35–38 a model for us?

Share the Heart of God

- Paul was a prisoner, yet on Malta he was setting everyone else free by healing the sick people on the island. His inner reality shaped the reality around him instead of the other way around. How can you cultivate your inner reality into something that releases a blessing wherever you go, no matter what circumstances you face?

- Interestingly, the Jews in Rome were anxious to hear Paul share because "people everywhere are speaking against [Christianity]." How can negative views of the Christian faith sometimes serve as an opportunity to share the heart of God?

CONSIDER THIS

Perhaps the greatest wonder of Peter's and Paul's lives is that they still impact us today. As you conclude this study, take time to let their example sink into your heart. Challenge yourself to think and dream big. Then ask the Holy Spirit to work through you as he worked through them. It is time for the Holy Spirit's acts to be made known once again through the lovers of God!

Encounter the Heart of God

The Passion Translation Bible is a new, heart-level translation that expresses God's fiery heart of love to this generation, using Hebrew, Greek, and Aramaic manuscripts and merging the emotion and life-changing truth of God's Word. If you are hungry for God and want to know him on a deeper level, The Passion Translation will help you encounter God's heart and discover what he has for your life.

The Passion Translation box set includes the following eight books:

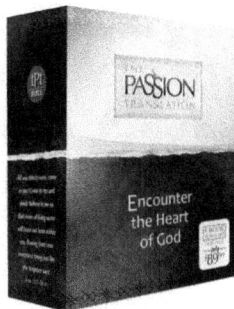

Psalms: Poetry on Fire
Proverbs: Wisdom from Above
Song of Songs: Divine Romance
Matthew: Our Loving King

John: Eternal Love
Luke and Acts: To the Lovers of God
Hebrews and James: Faith Works
Letters from Heaven: From the Apostle Paul (Galatians, Ephesians, Philippians, Colossians, I & II Timothy)

Additional titles available include:
Mark: Miracles and Mercy
Romans: Grace and Glory
1 & 2 Corinthians: Love and Truth

THE
PASSION
TRANSLATION

thePassionTranslation.com

Back Cover Material

The book of Acts picks up where Jesus' story left off in the gospel of Luke by exploring the continuing presence of Christ on earth through the church empowered by the Holy Spirit. This inspired account of church history will awaken your soul with transforming power and give you courage to be a witness for Christ wherever he sends you!

We've designed this study to help you explore and discover God's heart for the world through Luke's biography of history's most unlikely movement, the church of Jesus Christ. Each uniquely-crafted lesson opens with an introduction and key verse to reveal important themes. Four sections guide readers through Acts in a way that will help you discover, explore, experience, and share the heart of God more deeply.

Dive into this book heart first, to discover and experience the same fire that fueled the passion of early Christians two thousand years ago!

ABOUT THE PASSIONATE LIFE BIBLE STUDY SERIES

God longs for everyone to encounter the passion of his heart. Inspired by *The Passion Translation,* this heart-level Bible study is ideal for both individual devotional study and small groups. Kindle a burning desire for a passion-filled life fueled by the heart of God!